How to
Activate the
Hidden Power
In
Gemstones &
Crystals

Robert W Wood
(Diploma in Hypnotherapy)

Rosewood Publishing

First published in U.K. 2002
By Rosewood Publishing
P.O. Box 219, Huddersfield,
West Yorkshire HD2 2YT

www.rosewood-gifts.co.uk

Copyright © 2002

Revised cover and
Re-printed in 2011

Robert W Wood D.Hp
Asserts the moral right to be identified
As the author of this work

Copy-editing
Margaret Wakefield BA (Hons) London
www.euroreportage.co.uk

Cover photograph by
Robert W Wood D.Hp

Cover and layout re-designed by
AJ Typesetting
www.ajtype.co.uk

Printed in Great Britain by
Delta Design & Print Ltd
www.deltaleeds.co.uk

ISBN 978-0-9532930-6-3   BK7

The most powerful word for 'healing' on earth

**'We can see and feel the rays of the sun
but not the power that created it.'**

**With time, help and patience,
we are learning to see the unseen,
to hear and understand that which cannot be heard,
and to speak that which is unspoken.**

Our fascination with Gemstones and Crystals

How often I've heard people say, "But what do I do with them?" I answer: "You have to connect with them." "But how?" So this book is dedicated to answering that question: "How?" Our journey starts at the very beginning. It's only here that we will discover how this fascination with Gemstones and Crystals started, and where the information came from.

It began...

Starting at the beginning means going back in time to the creation of planet Earth and our solar system. Earth was formed around 4,500 million years ago, and all the building blocks of the Universe are captured here on Earth. Our Earth is over 80% 'crystal', the crust being largely silicon and oxygen; and, when combined with six common elements - Sodium, Aluminium, Calcium, Iron, Magnesium and Potassium - this 'chemical cocktail' helped to produce the building blocks for our world. With this cocktail came an amazing variety of Gemstones and Crystals in all kinds of shapes, sizes and colours.

What are Crystals?

They are of mineral substance, and their molecular composition is arranged and geometrically fixed. When you look at a crystal you can see many different sides or 'faces', angles, planes and points. The word 'crystal' comes from the Greek word 'krystallos' meaning 'ice'. The Greeks gave the name believing that crystals were ice, frozen. Crystalline materials as diverse as sugar, metal, salt - even our teeth - have all got one thing in common: an ordered internal structure of a regularly-repeating three-dimensional pattern. Even the most irregular or misshapen crystal shares this atomical neatness. A crystal's external shape is dependent on its specific chemical ingredients, the way the atoms are linked together, and the conditions prevailing at the time of growth. There are many different permutations, producing a wide variation in shapes, colour and hardness.

Colour.

The majority of crystals contain 'rogue' atoms - minute impurities, usually metal, within their chemical structure. These trace elements, or impurities, contribute to the wide range of colours. As a general rule of thumb: the greater the amount of trace impurities contained within the crystal, the deeper the colour. There are some crystals, such as agate and jasper, which we call Gemstones. These contain the same atomic structure, but, unlike crystal, their form is not visible to the naked eye and they appear to be ordinary coloured stones without geometric form, just like pebbles from a beach. Only by using a microscope is it possible to see the thousands of little crystals of which they are composed.

Crystal electricity.

Certain crystals, most notably the Quartz family, can convert mechanical pressure into electrical energy. To demonstrate this, take two quartz crystals - rock crystal, rose quartz or amethyst will do - and rub them together in the dark. You'll see them light up quite spectacularly. It's called a 'piezoelectric' effect, from the Greek word 'piezo' meaning 'I press'. If you have a gas oven you may have used a special lighter-wand to create a spark. This special tool has a piece of quartz built into it, which releases energy (the spark) when it is used, and it works without the need of a battery. While natural quartz is abundant, it is rarely perfect, with all its 'rogue' trace elements rendering it unsuitable for commercial use. So piezoelectric crystals are produced synthetically in the laboratory. Although synthetic, they still have the same atomic structure and properties as their natural counterparts.

A Quartz Watch.

Why is there a quartz in a watch? The answer is, because quartz makes a timepiece so accurate, to within only a second or two a year - and that's accurate. So how does it work? Scientists discovered that the atoms within a micro-thin slice of synthetic quartz (such as is ideal for clocks and watches) vibrate at 32,768 times per second. The crystal requires very little power, and this is often supplied by a very tiny battery. As the atoms in the quartz vibrate they emit very precise electronic pulses. These pulses are then channelled through microchip circuitry, where they are successively halved in a series of 15 steps. The result is really astounding: it produces a single, constant pulse per second. Which is why watches and clocks are now so accurate.

From science to the 'mysteries'.

Even earliest man found gemstones and crystals attractive and colourful, and used them for jewellery; but at the same time there was another interest developing, and this more to do with their 'magical attraction', rather than their looks. It's not difficult to understand their fascination, when you think about the piezoelectric effect: stones that light up.

I think it's strange that even to-day, things don't seem to have changed that much. On one hand we have the geologists, who will drool over a lovely piece of crystal and talk about its shape, its symmetry, its inclusions and how it looks. On the other hand, we have the New Age followers - crystal healers and the alternative therapists - all drooling over the same piece and explaining how it feels, describing its energy, its power and what it can do.

A mystical journey, a brief history.

In pre-historic times, people were nomadic, always on the move. Then about 6000 years ago, early man began to settle down and build himself more permanent homes, and he started keeping animals and growing crops. These early civilisations, such as the Babylonians, Egyptians and Chinese, began to believe that the stars and planets that they could see so clearly in the night skies, influenced their lives. The Babylonians, in particular, thought that the position of the stars represented coded messages from the gods. Their priests, holy men and sages spent much of their time studying these so-called messages with great care, observing and plotting the night sky. Studying in this way produced a science that we now know as Astrology.

The Egyptian Connection.

Here's a mystery that won't go away. The Egyptians have had a love affair for thousands of years with the brightest star in the sky. It's called 'Sirius', and according to their mythology it represents their goddess Isis. The great pyramid at Gizeh was believed to have been built because of an ancient knowledge connecting planet Earth with the Sirius star system, often referred to as the Dog Star. In the pyramid it's been discovered that there are various chambers or rooms. These have been named the Kings, the Queens and the Lower Chambers. These chambers have tiny passages, like windows, leading to the outside of the pyramid; and on rare occasions, at intervals which may stretch across thousands of years, there are times when, if you were in the chamber looking out, you would witness a perfect alignment with various star systems, including the star Sirius. What it all means still remains a mystery.

Spaceships.

Some Chinese stone discs were discovered, and when the inscriptions on them were translated, they told of a crashed spaceship from the same star system Sirius. Even more curious is a unique ceremony practised only by the African tribe, Dogon. They tell the legend of the Nommos, who arrived in a vessel along with fire and thunder. The Nommos could live on land, but dwelled mostly in the sea. Similar creatures have been noted in other ancient civilisations, including Egypt's goddess Isis.

The African Tribe - Dogon.

It seems that the Dogon tribe knew a lot about the star system Sirius, including the existence of a smaller star called Sirius B. Both these are well outside our own solar system, and it's impossible to see the smaller star with the naked eye; so this begs the question: How did they know? A photo of this smaller star was not obtained until 1970. Yet the Dogon tribe had revealed their knowledge of the Sirius star system to a French anthropologist in 1930. It's even been suggested that this information is more than 5000 years old and was possessed by the ancient Egyptians before 3200 BC - well before the Pyramids. The Dogon also claimed that a third star existed in the Sirius system, and around it orbited a planet from which the Nommos came. This Sirius mystery has now changed dramatically. Why? Because in the year 1995 two French astronomers, Daniel Benest and J.L. Duvent, published the results of years of study, and for the very first time confirmed the existence of this third star.

**Six thousand years ago, ancient man had
a knowledge that modern man is only just rediscovering.**

Rather than go deeper into the unknown, let's discover what we do know.

Cause and Effect.

Can a lump of rock really do anything? Can it heal, change luck, and give more energy? The simple answer, you may be surprised to know, is: Yes, it can. There is a 'law of cause and effect'; this is the underpinning bedrock of the Universe. It's also a very useful protector whenever you come across something you can't understand or explain, because you know that there is an explanation, even if you can't see one at the time. Understanding this gives you control over your mind, but especially your imagination.

**Let's not look at 'if they can', but more 'how they can'.
We often see the effect; let's look for the cause.**

You wouldn't dream of entering a room at night without first putting the light on. The power's there; you just need to turn it on. Using this analogy: if the lights didn't go on (that's the 'effect'), what could be the cause? It could be that the light bulb is broken. Solution: change it. Or it could be that you haven't paid the bill and have been cut off: pay it. Now turn this around. You need a light bulb that's working - your 'crystal'; the electricity to be on - 'the hidden power'; and someone to switch it on - 'you'.

Expand your mind.

Who could believe that an aeroplane full of passengers, loaded with tons of fuel, could fly? It seems impossible - but it does. Or that a ship made out of steel can float? But it does. It's impossible; but it does. We now believe it because we see it; and because we can see it, we believe it. Now imagine, for a moment, that you didn't know about planes, and all you could see was the vapour trail in the sky. Without the mental anchor of 'cause and effect', what would your mind, and especially your imagination, make of it? It would run riot. You would feel anxious, nervous - not understanding causes unease; but the moment someone says, "That's an aeroplane you're looking at, they take off and land at airports," - the fact that someone else seems to know what an aeroplane is, can be quite reassuring. And so knowledge, wherever it comes from, moves us from a state of anxiety to calm and serenity.

A solid foundation.

How did we get from earth science into a world of 'magic'? What happened? The answer is, 'Man' happened. It is only Man who can take an abstract and work with it. He is responsible for adding the one ingredient that's so powerful, it can't and won't be held back; nothing on earth can stop it; and one day it may be shown that it is the very reason for life itself.

In the beginning was the word, and the word was with God, through him all things were made; without him nothing was made that has been made. Then the word became flesh and lived.

Is the Genie out of the bottle? Let me tell you not what it is, but where it is. What you are discovering forms the first step towards activating your crystals. This is the first foundation of your knowledge: that which we are seeking will be found in the 'mind' - but where in the mind? It's in the part called the 'subconscious'. Before I tell you where in the subconscious, let me show you, using words and pictures, your subconscious.

The subconscious.

First of all, the good news is that we all have a subconscious, because we all have a mind. Whether we choose to use it or not mainly depends on ourselves. Our minds are likened to the most powerful computers on earth, and it's nobody's fault except our own if we choose not to use it. In my mind it's a free gift from the Creator and it's ours to use. Some may say, "But my brain isn't any good, I failed at school." I promise you it is, especially for what you are about to discover.

There are two main parts to the brain, our mind. One's the conscious, and the other the subconscious. The conscious acts like a 'gatekeeper'. It controls what is allowed in. Imagine the largest stately home in the world, set in thousands of acres, employing tens of thousands of people from all walks of life and backgrounds - and the only access is past the gatekeeper. That's how the mind works. Another analogy could be the captain of the world's largest ship - the captain representing the conscious, and all the workers below decks representing the subconscious. Sadly, if the captain decided to run aground, the crew wouldn't stop him. It's important to bear this in mind. The power to direct is in the conscious part, but the power to achieve is held within the subconscious. So make sure they're both going in the right direction.

When two or more are together I am there. I tell you that if two of you on earth agree about anything you ask for, it will be done for you by my Father in Heaven.
MATT. 18: 19-20

The greatest computer of then all.

Those of you who can drive a car will understand this. When you can drive, you 'consciously' decide where you are going - "I'm going from here to there" - but you cannot drive a car 'consciously'. You drive it 'automatically'; that is, through the subconscious. If you want to know what I mean, just look at a learner trying to drive a car consciously, having to think about the clutch, handbrake, mirrors, signals and brakes. When they are thinking about it, it's difficult and awkward. But the moment the subconscious kicks in, not only can they drive using all the instruments available, they are also able to read the road, see dangers and possible problems and at the same time compute situations that may never arise; and all this is being done every microsecond (one millionth of a second). And if that doesn't blow your mind, then think about this: while all this is happening, they are more than capable of holding a conversation. Wow! There isn't a computer on this planet that can drive a car and I don't think there ever will be. So who are we?

There is another way of showing you your subconscious other than in words, and that is with pictures. On page 17 there is a picture of a woman. Just look at it, and after a while the picture will change. This effect is your subconscious having to reveal itself; because there are two pictures in one, and basically the subconscious is saying to the conscious, "I can't make up my mind, see what you think." So the picture will continue to change backwards and forwards, forcing your subconscious to reveal itself.

The Imagination.

The power to connect to all things is within the mind, and you are now beginning to understand just how powerful your mind really is. Not only can it drive a car, but it can also transmit and receive thoughts, a little like the way the Internet works. Within the subconscious lies the greatest power of them all - the Imagination. Once you have discovered how to turn this 'program' on - and you will - then activating the 'hidden power' in gemstones and crystals becomes child's play.

Another way of experiencing and explaining the power of imagination: have you ever gone to pick up a telephone that's been ringing, only to find yourself feeling that you somehow know who it is, and when you pick up the phone you discover you were right? It's commonly called 'telepathy' ('a communication between people of thoughts, feelings etc involving mechanisms that cannot be understood in terms of known scientific laws'). I think that it's because the person making the phone call knows you and, whilst they are dialling or thinking about dialling, they are forming an image; in other words, they are imagining you. This is probably done without thinking; but it's this image that somehow gets transmitted, and you are the one who picks up on it.

A secret code.
It doesn't matter if the person phoning lives half way around the world, you can still experience it. And what can travel so fast around the world? The Internet can. However, there is a secret code. Understand this and activating your crystal really will be 'child's play'. It's this: whenever you use your power of imagination to seek, attract, achieve, change or heal, you have to add one more ingredient, and this ingredient is vital.

I once used this formula so effectively that the results could only be described as spectacular. I bought and removed a 'mountain'. Yes, you read it right. Why a mountain? Because I thought, if I could remove it - the mountain, that is - then I might be able to build houses on the site. And I did. I removed a mountain and built houses. How did I do it? I used the same principles found in this book. You'll have to read my book 'Discover Why Crystal Healing Works' to read the full story (copies available from the publishers, their name is on the back cover). Believe me, with this vital ingredient you can move mountains; I did. And the secret is this: whenever you visualise your dream, your goal or desire, you have to add one more thing. You have to add feeling or an emotion. It makes a difference. It seems to energise the thought.

Jesus said, "Therefore I tell you, whatever you ask for in prayer, believe that you have received it, and it will be yours."

How do you believe you have received something? Imagine you already have it; see it in your mind's eye; and then imagine how would you feel if you did have it. The feeling helps to energise the thought. This is also a formulation for prayer. The 'power of prayer' is real; but change the expression to the 'power of thought', and the power comes back to where it should be: within each and everyone of us. It's not exclusive to a church, although you'll find it there. I did.

Imagining a feeling is not that difficult, but you do have to know the difference between seeing in your mind's eye and feeling it. How would you feel if you won the lottery, or were told by a doctor that you were expecting, after years of trying to conceive? if you found a new career, or were offered a promotion? if you were healed, or told you were in remission? It's the difference between watching an erotic film, as compared to being in it.

A coincidence.
I believe there is a coded language; so whenever I hear someone say, "You won't believe this," or, "That's strange," or, "I was just thinking about you," or, "That's a coincidence," I always listen to what comes next - because this is the hidden power at work. We have all been giving 'free will', and this allows us to dismiss this power. And how do we dismiss it? - we call it 'a coincidence'.

An example of this way of thinking is the following story: Whilst I was walking through town on a Friday afternoon, I had what I thought was a great idea. If only I could find that picture, what a lovely way to finish my talks and presentations! I called into a specialist bookshop and described this picture to them. To my relief the assistant seemed to know what I was talking about. But then the bombshell: "I know what you mean, but I haven't a clue where you'll find it," he said. So I left the shop with a feeling of disappointment. I thought at the time that it would have been a brilliant idea.

On Saturday and even Sunday I still felt this disappointment, but by Monday I seemed to have forgotten all about it. That is, until my daughter came in from work and told me how a friend of hers had been to a car boot sale the previous day and had bought what she thought was a very unusual tapestry. In fact it was so unusual that she (my daughter) tried to draw me a picture of it, because she thought I might find it interesting. When I looked, I couldn't believe my eyes. It was the same picture I had tried to find three days earlier in the specialist bookshop. Now was that a coincidence, or not?

The same picture is at the top of page three. If you haven't already noticed, the word is upside down; and if you need a clue - look into the light, not the dark, and you'll see it. It's the most powerful name on earth that I know for representing love, hope, peace and understanding, and the power to heal.

I had gone into the shop, which was a Christian bookshop, and described the picture to the assistant whilst at the same time I was imagining it. I was seeing it in my mind's eye. That's how we think: we see pictures, symbols and images. So I imagined it; then I added a feeling. In this case, surprisingly, it was a feeling of disappointment. It's this extra ingredient - a feeling - that seems to help.

Why not try out the following experiment: look at your phone and imagine it ringing. Hear the tone within your mind. Then imagine answering it, and it being someone you would like to hear from. Then imagine how would you feel if it was them. Energise it. It's this that seems to make the difference. If the person you have imagined, with feeling, lives halfway around the world and calls you, it could save you a fortune on phone bills. If you find you are good at this, and I know many people who are, then everybody will be calling you; and often when they do call they will start the conversation by saying something like "I just had this thought that I should give you a call." Try it - it works.

The hidden power.
The 'hidden power' is another name many would give to the 'Universal Life Force'. It's representative of the energy that created the Universe. Many may call it God. Like an artist - you know he existed by the pictures he painted. And where do you find the 'God' of today? You'll find him in each and every one of us. All this could be likened to making a phone call. If you know the person's number, you can ring them anywhere in the world; all you have to do is own a phone, make sure it's turned on, and dial the number, and that's all there is to it.

Now imagine all the things that have to be in place for us to make the call. The person on the other end has to have a phone and it has to be turned on. We need the engineers and the scientists who build the systems; the satellites; the cables; the motivation, the energy and the imagination - all the ingredients that represent 'Power for life'. Discover for yourselves the hidden power. It's real and you are now learning how to activate it.

Four simple steps.
With our newly-found basic knowledge, and with the help of our wisdom and understanding, let's activate and connect with the hidden power. It's the same power that can be found in the creation of Gemstones and Crystal. Our first step is to select; the second is to cleanse; the third is to connect; and the fourth, to visualise and finally to receive.

12

Step one.

Start by selecting the crystal or gemstone you want. It will be the one that represents your desire, aims or goals. To help, there is a list of gemstones and crystals on page fifteen. Here you'll find the most popular gemstones and crystals, plus our own unique range of 'power gems'. These have been designed around titles, rather than stones - for example, 'Good Luck' or 'Energy Booster'. There's the 'Healer', or 'To remove aches and pains'; or you may be looking for 'Peace of Mind'. You may be thinking of an Amethyst to help you sleep, or the 'Adults Only' to keep you awake; whatever the need, there'll be a gemstone that can help.

Step two.

Next we need to clean them. Why? Because there are many who believe that stones can carry both positive and negative energy, and because you don't know where the stones have been. It won't do them any harm, so, to be safe, we clean them. It's a little like the body's DNA, but in this case it's the stone that's holding the memory. So, to neutralise any adverse effects, we cleanse them. You can, if you wish, just wash them or hold them under a running tap; I've heard of some placing them into a stream for a few minutes; you can even bury them in the ground for 24 hours to allow Mother Nature to re-energise them, and then wash them. In fact, the more you do, and the more ritualistic it is, the better they seem to work. There are as many ways as you can imagine. In my research I have never come across a right or wrong way: just find the way that feels comfortable for you, and it will be your 'right way'.

Step three.

Next you have to connect with them. Don't be confused; this is a mental exercise. You are now going to draw upon all that 'personal computer power' that's held within the brain; you're going to focus and energise your thoughts to connect. At its simplest, you could just wear one, or carry it in your pocket or purse. You could make or buy a pouch to carry them in. My mother at a craft fair told of how she had got one of the lucky lottery stones (Green Aventurine, it's said to be a money magnet), and although she said she hadn't yet won, she found that ever since she had carried it in her purse she had never felt short of money. Since hearing this I've always carried a Green Aventurine in my pocket. Here is the point: if that stone now went missing, I would know about it. Why? Because I know I am now connected to it.

I remember at one display I lost my stone. I looked high and low for it. I even moved the furniture. Anyone watching would have thought I'd lost the Crown Jewels. Just as I was leaving I realised the only place I hadn't looked was under the piano. So I went back, moved the piano, and yes - you've guessed - the stone was there. So was I connected or not?

If you buy a Gemstone or Crystal and bring it home, put it into a drawer and forget about it, you're not connected. You have to find your way of interacting with it. If you carried a stone or crystal, and it got lost, and you didn't notice, then you were not connected. But if you did notice and started to look for it, then you were connected. Are you getting the idea? It's like the difference between a mother and a babysitter. The babysitter only connects with the child for the duration of the time she's 'sitting', whereas the mother is always connected, even when she goes out and leaves the child in the hands of the babysitter.

Step four.
Now you are connected, you have to use the greatest power of all. It's your imagination that holds the key. You now have to visualise what you want from your crystal; you have to see the end result. This is like going into a railway station and asking for a ticket. The station master will ask you where you want to go, and if you say you don't know, then you have missed the point. However, if you can say exactly what you want, then you are really more than halfway there.

The purpose of visualisation is a little like making a phone call to a helpline that's only got an answering machine. It means you are going to do all the talking - or in this case, the 'imagining'. You hope and believe that eventually someone will listen, and will then help. The only difference is that when they do 'listen', it's not to words, but to images and thoughts: your visualisation.

For example, if you would like to become pregnant, then select a Moonstone (said to be good for childbearing and fertility), wash it, and then, whilst holding it, imagine your desired outcome. Imagine the midwife saying, "Congratulations - it's a boy!" Now here is the key: Imagine, at the same time, how would you feel if it happened. Energise the thought by adding a feeling. In church it's called the 'power of prayer', and it's real. Expect a result; in fact, be surprised if you don't get one. Never let go or stop living in hope. You can change the future by changing the way you think. Tomorrow is still to come. Make the call, and let Universal Law take care of the rest; and be overjoyed when it does. Be prepared to receive.

Although the following information is not authoritative,
it is a fluid interpretation from many sources.
Any information given in this book is not intended to be taken as a replacement
for medical advice. Any person with a condition requiring medical attention
should consult a qualified doctor or therapist.
On no account should a gemstone or crystal ever be swallowed.

RED JASPER A powerful healing stone. Can help those suffering from emotional problems; its power to give strength and console such sufferers is well known. Good for: kidneys, bladder. Improves the sense of smell.

ROSE QUARTZ Healing qualities for the mind. Gives help with migraine and headaches. Good for: spleen, kidneys and circulatory system. Coupled with Hematite, works wonders on aches and pains throughout the body. Lifts spirits and dispels negative thoughts.

BLACK ONYX Can give a sense of courage, and helps to discover truth. Instils calm and serenity. Good for: bone marrow, relief of stress.

MOTHER OF PEARL Aptly dubbed the sea of tranquillity. Calms the nerves. Good for: calcified joints, digestive system.

TIGER EYE The 'confidence stone'. Inspires brave but sensible behaviour. Good for: liver, kidneys, bladder. Invigorates and energises.

CARNELIAN A very highly-evolved healer. Good for: rheumatism, depression, neuralgia. Helps regularise the menstrual cycle.

GREEN AVENTURINE Stabilises through inspiring independence. Acts as a general tonic. Good for: skin conditions; losing anxiety and fears.

RHODONITE Improves the memory; reduces stress. Good for: emotional trauma, mental breakdown; spleen, kidneys, heart and blood.

SODALITE Imparts youth and freshness. Calms and clears the mind. When combined with Rhodonite, can produce the 'Elixir of Life'.

OBSIDIAN SNOWFLAKE A powerful healer. Brings insight and understanding, wisdom and love. Good for: eyesight, stomach and intestines.

BLUE AGATE Improves the ego. A stone of strength and courage; a supercharger of energy. Good for: stress, certain ear disorders.

AMETHYST Aids creative thinking. Relieves insomnia when placed under pillow. Good for: blood pressure, fits, grief and insomnia.

HEMATITE A very optimistic inspirer of courage and magnetism. Lifts gloominess. Good for: blood, spleen; generally strengthens the body.

ROCK CRYSTAL Enlarges the aura of everything near to it and acts as a catalyst to increase the healing powers of other minerals. Good for: brain, soul; dispels negativity in your own energy field.

MOONSTONE Gives inspiration and enhances the emotions. Good for: period pain and kindred disorders, fertility and childbearing.

o0o

Power Gems.
A unique group of Gemstones and Crystals, carefully linked in harmony to unite their individual mystic powers and provide a holistic force which can revive health, increase wealth, bring peace and provide energy.

HEALER - Carnelian, Red Jasper and Rock Crystal.

GOOD LUCK - Obsidian Snowflake, Green Aventurine and Moonstone.

PEACE OF MIND - Green Aventurine, Rose Quartz and Rhodonite.

FOR WILLPOWER - Rose Quartz, Black Onyx and Rock Crystal.

ADULTS ONLY - Rose Quartz, Amethyst and Carnelian.

TO REMOVE ACHES & PAINS: Rose Quartz, Hematite and Rock Crystal.

ELIXIR OF LIFE - Rhodonite and Sodalite.

ENERGY BOOSTER - Carnelian, Amethyst and Rock Crystal.

IMAGINE - Rose Quartz, Amethyst and Green Aventurine.

FERTILITY - Moonstone, Rose Quartz and Rock Crystal.

CONFIDENCE - Tiger Eye, Green Aventurine and Black Onyx.

Leeper's Ambiguous Lady
"My Wife My Mother-in-Law' (first published November 6th 1915)

Can you see an attractive young lady or an old witch?
Objectively they are both present in the picture,
but it is impossible to see them both together.

See your local stockist for any Gemstones and Crystals mentioned in this publication. However, if you are having difficulty in obtaining any of the stones mentioned, we do offer our own mail order service and would be more than pleased to supply any of the stones listed.

For further details - write to:
ROSEWOOD,
P.O. Box 219. Huddersfield, West Yorkshire. HD2 2YT

E-mail enquiries to: info@rosewood-gifts.co.uk

Or why not visit our website for even more information:
www.rosewood-gifts.co.uk

Other titles in the 'POWER FOR LIFE' series:

Discover your own Special Birthstone and the renowned Healing Powers of Crystals REF. (BK1) A look at Birthstones, personality traits and characteristics associated with each Sign of the Zodiac – plus a guide to the author's own unique range of Power Gems.

A Special Glossary of Healing Stones plus Birthstones REF. (BK2) An introduction to Crystal Healing, with an invaluable Glossary listing common ailments and suggesting combinations of Gemstones/Crystals.

Create a Wish Kit using a Candle, a Crystal and the Imagination of Your Mind REF. (BK3) 'The key to happiness is having dreams; the key to success is making dreams come true.' This book will help you achieve.

Gemstone & Crystal Elixirs – Potions for Love, Health, Wealth, Energy and Success REF. (BK4) An ancient form of 'magic', invoking super-natural powers. You won't believe the power you can get from a drink!

Crystal Pendulum for Dowsing REF. (BK5) An ancient knowledge for unlocking your Psychic Power, to seek out information not easily available by any other means. Contains easy-to-follow instructions.

Crystal Healing – Fact or Fiction? Real or Imaginary? REF. (BK6) Find the answer in this book. Discover a hidden code used by Jesus Christ for healing, and read about the science of light and colour. It's really amazing.

Astrology: The Secret Code REF. (BK8) In church it's called 'Myers Briggs typology'. In this book it's called 'psychological profiling'. If you read your horoscope, you need to read this to find your true birthstone.

Talismans, Charms and Amulets REF. (BK9) Making possible the powerful transformations which we would not normally feel empowered to do without a little extra help. Learn how to make a lucky talisman.

A Guide to the Mysteries surrounding Gemstones & Crystals REF. (BK10) Crystal healing, birthstones, crystal gazing, lucky talismans, elixirs, crystal dowsing, astrology, rune stones, amulets and rituals.

A Simple Guide to Gemstone & Crystal Power – a mystical A-Z of stones REF. (BK11) From Agate to Zircon, all you ever needed or wanted to know about the mystical powers of gemstones and crystals.

Change Your Life by Using the Most Powerful Crystal on Earth REF. (BK12) The most powerful crystal on earth can be yours. A book so disarmingly simple to understand, yet with a tremendous depth of knowledge.

All the above books are available from your local stockist,
or, if not, from the publisher.

NOTES

Welcome to the world of Rosewood

An extract from a 'thank- you' letter for one of my books.

"I realised just how much you really had indeed understood me and my need for direction and truly have allowed me the confidence and strength to know and believe I can achieve whatever I want in life"

If you like natural products, hand-crafted gifts including Gemstone jewellery, objects of natural beauty – the finest examples from Mother Nature, tinged with an air of Mystery – then we will not disappoint you. For those who can enjoy that feeling of connection with the esoteric nature of Gemstones and Crystals, then our 'Power for Life – Power Bracelets could be ideal for you. Each bracelet comes with its own guide explaining a way of thinking that's so powerful it will change your life and the information comes straight from the Bible. e.g. read Mark 11: 22

We regularly give inspirational talks on Crystal Power – fact or fiction? A captivating story about the world's fascination with natural gemstones and crystals and how the Placebo effect explains the healing power of gemstones and crystals – it's intriguing. And it's available on a CD

To see our full range of books, jewellery and gifts including CD's and DVD'S

Visit our web site - www.rosewood-gifts.co.uk

To see our latest videos go to 'You Tube' and type in Rosewood Gifts.